W9-CFE-126

DISCARD

HIJACKING & SECURITY

FIGHTING TERRORISM

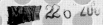

David Baker

PORTAGE COUNTY DISTRICT LIBRARY
AURORA MEMORIAL BRANCH
115 EAST PIONEER TRAIL
AURORA, OH 44202

PORTAGE COUNTY DISTRICT LIBRARY
10482 SOUTH STREET
GARRETTSVILLE, OH 44231

Rourke
Publishing LLC
Vero Beach, Florida 32964

© 2006 Rourke Publishing LLC

All rights reserved. No part of this book may be reproduced or utilized in any form or by any means, electronic or mechanical including photocopying, recording, or by any information storage and retrieval system without permission in writing from the publisher.

www.rourkepublishing.com

PHOTO CREDITS: pp. 24, 25: AFP/Getty Images; p. 35: Yasser Al-Zayyat/AFP/Getty Images; p. 28: Bettmann/Corbis; pp. 34, 41: Department of Defense; pp. 37 (Gene Corley), 42 (Andrea Booher): F.E.M.A; p. 33: Dirck Halstead/Time Life Pictures/Getty Images; p. 17: Hulton Archive/Getty Images; p. 10: Nabil Ismail/AFP/Getty Images; p. 16: Carl Iwasaki/Time Life Pictures/Getty Images; pp. 6, 22: Keystone/Getty Images; pp. 5, 13 (Wilbur & Orville Wright), 15 (F. S. A./Office of War Information Photo Collection), 19: Library of Congress; p. 7: Peter Macdiarmid/Getty Images; p. 29: Stan Meagher/Express/Getty Images; pp. 12, 20: NASA; p. 32: Newsmakers/Getty Images; p. 39: Paul J. Richards/AFP/Getty Images; p. 18: Jake Schoellkopf/Getty Images; p. 26: David Silverman/Getty Images; pp. 11, 30: Transport Security Administration; pp. 4, 31 (James Tourtellotte), 8 (Gerald L. Nino): U.S. Customs & Border Protection; p. 38 (Photographer's Mate 1st Class Michael W. Pendergrass): U.S. Navy

Title page picture shows a security officer examing a scan of an airport passenger's luggage.

Produced for Rourke Publishing by Discovery Books
Editor: Paul Humphrey
Designer: Ian Winton
Photo researcher: Rachel Tisdale

Library of Congress Cataloging-in-Publication Data

Baker, David, 1944-
  Hijacking and security / by David Baker.
     p. cm. -- (Fighting terrorism)
  Includes index.
  ISBN 1-59515-488-4
  1. Terrorism--United States--Prevention--Juvenile literature. 2. War on Terrorism, 2001---Juvenile literature. 3. September 11 Terrorist Attacks, 2001--Juvenile literature. 4. Terrorism--History--Juvenile literature. I. Title. II. Series.
  HV6432.B34 2006
  363.32--dc22
                                   2005028008

Printed in the USA

TABLE OF CONTENTS

Chapter One

The Price of Terror

Terrorists have been around since the history of civilization and nations began. There have always been people who wish to use force and aggression to **coerce**, blackmail, and terrorize civilians and innocent bystanders to exert political or religious force. Within the last century national leaders such as Adolf Hitler and Joseph Stalin used terrorism to **suppress** opposition and crush other parties in their bid for power. Once installed as leaders, they continued to survive only because of the fear they brought to their subjects.

Adolf Hitler used terror to suppress the freedoms of the German people during the 1930s and 1940s.

In the Soviet Union Stalin used what would today be defined as terrorism and **genocide** to stay in power, setting up labor camps and slave work factories. In Germany, Hitler came to power and used terrorist tactics to create a sense of **subservience**. In the

(Left) The worst terrorist outrage in history. The debris from the collapsed Twin Towers in New York City, September 2001.

Freedom fighters struggle against tyrannical rulers and attempt to free themselves and their fellow citizens from oppression. The division between terrorists and freedom fighters is sometimes hard to define. Terrorists seek to gain by violence and aggression against people outside their own country changes that they demand should be made to their society or the lands to which they were born. In non-democratic countries it is sometimes necessary to take up arms against a rogue government. There is never any excuse for terrorism.

majority of people nestled the hope that some day things would change. This is one form of terrorism every bit as real as the one we face today.

Today's terrorism is as much the enemy of democracy and freedom as were Hitler's Nazi Germany and Stalin's communist Soviet Union. In some countries around the world people are frustrated because the changes they seek are either not happening fast enough or not happening at all. They want instant solutions to problems that have been around for decades, perhaps

Terrorist or freedom fighter? To many, Cuban revolutionary Che Guevara was a violent terrorist, but others saw him as a freedom fighter.

Acts of terrorism can take place anywhere. This bus in the British capital of London was destroyed by terrorists in July 2005.

centuries. Often these people have expectations far beyond reality. Some seek to change things in a democratic and peaceful way. Others, however, are determined that the changes they

Secretary Tom Ridge announcing the new seal of the Department of Homeland Security. This new government department was formed in 2003 to help counter terrorist acts in the United States.

seek will happen despite opposition or resistance. They use any means at their disposal to threaten and cajole, turning to mass terrorism and the use of modern technology to generate hate, violence, and murder.

In doing this terrorists become the **perpetrators** of the wrongs they seek to put right. In reality, of course, there is no justification. No major religion allows the use of force except in self-defense, and those who claim to have a religious, moral, or political right to carry out terrorist acts are unable to find any **legitimate** reason for their actions.

Chapter Two

The New Terror Weapons

Terrorists have used just about every piece of modern invention and technology application to carry out their destructive aims. They seek to gain maximum effect from their actions. This includes getting the widest publicity as well as the most effective ways of bringing pressure through terrorism on those they select as their enemies. They have no uniforms, belong to no legitimate political systems, and have no moral, ethical, or religious base for their actions.

Terrorists have historically sought to increase the effectiveness of their actions using guns, trains, cars, ships, and aircraft to expand both the effect and the publicity through fear. Airplane hijacking is close to the top of any fear priority list.

Even without the threat of terrorism, flying causes fear in a lot of people. Since the terrorist outrage of September 11, 2001, this fear has been magnified by the possibility that the airliner you are flying on could fall into the hands of fanatical terrorists. Suddenly the fear of flying has taken on a completely new and powerful emotion.

An Islamic terrorist holding a machine gun leaves the hijacked TWA flight 847 at Beirut Airport, Lebanon, June 1985.

To the terrorist, you are the perfect victim. Paralyzed by the fear of imminent death, totally unable to change the situation, you are at the mercy of mad people, for whom death for them is believed to be a welcome step toward a better life in the hereafter.

Before September 11, 2001 the majority of hijackers wanted to force a crew at gunpoint to fly to a destination of their choice for some political or criminal purpose. Fortunately, the majority of hijackings are still for this purpose and do not always mean a loss of life. Sadly, the hijackings of 9/11 were altogether different.

The hijackers took control of aircraft to deliberately fly them into buildings to increase the death toll or the dramatic impact of their action. The events of 9/11 demonstrated in the most dramatic way the impact and the horror generated worldwide by the deaths of more than 3,000 people on a single day of terror unlike anything before. It must

Routine scanning of all passengers' baggage has made airplane travel safer today than at any time in its history.

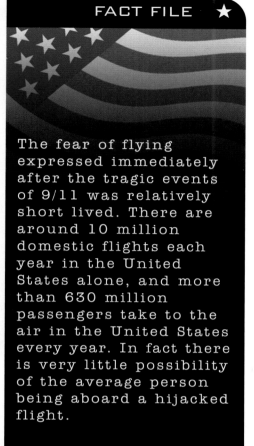

FACT FILE ★

The fear of flying expressed immediately after the tragic events of 9/11 was relatively short lived. There are around 10 million domestic flights each year in the United States alone, and more than 630 million passengers take to the air in the United States every year. In fact there is very little possibility of the average person being aboard a hijacked flight.

The smoke from the attacks on the World Trade Center in New York City on September 11, 2001, could be seen from space.

also be remembered that this attack was the first incident of international terrorism through hijacking on American soil.

Hijackings take place for a wide variety of reasons, but they all follow one of two **principles**. The first principle is that the hijacker seeks to achieve a result that he or she feels is impossible to attain in any other way. This can be to seek **refuge** in another country, to bring pressure for political change, or to shock with outrageous or unprecedented atrocity.

The second principle, sometimes included with the first, is that the hijacker needs to obtain the maximum attention for a cause or to protest against some religious or political group. Whatever the cause, such terrorist actions employ what began as the benign use of a new invention for public convenience and for travel early in the 20th century.

When Wilbur and Orville Wright made the world's first powered flight at Kitty Hawk, North Carolina, in December 1903, they could not have understood how far their invention would go. From flights lasting a few seconds possible only in light wind carrying two people at most, aviation has grown into a mass people mover—statistically the safest form of transportation ever invented.

In some ways it is surprising that aviation was left alone by international terrorists for so long. In the first 45 years of aviation history, there were only a few isolated incidents involving hijackings or piracy. By the end of the 1940s, however, a new age of **global** air travel ushered in an equally **escalating** incidence of terrorism in the skies. It was clearly only a matter of time before the airplane was used by terrorists and, inevitably, as a missile for mass destruction and death on a scale unimagined by the early pioneers of air transportation.

The first flight by Orville Wright in December 1903. Neither Orville nor his brother, Wilbur could have imagined that their invention would be used by terrorists to kill innocent people.

Chapter Three

The First Hijackers

The first recorded hijacking took place in February 1931 when Peruvian rebels seized a Pan American Airways mail plane with the object of dropping leaflets over Lima. The aircraft was a Fokker F.VII, a metal monoplane designed by the man who built some of the most famous German fighters of World War I (1914-1918). The aircraft could carry only eight passengers in addition to the two-man crew. The event went off without drama and was not repeated.

By the end of the decade World War II had broken out, and all international flights were cancelled or curtailed. When the war ended in 1945, the United States had a large number of long-range transport aircraft that were no longer needed to carry troops and equipment. Instead they were used to provide air transportation for passengers now able to travel across the Atlantic and Pacific oceans.

Air travel is now so much a part of everyday life that it is difficult to imagine the time when there were just a few flights each day and only a few each week across the world's oceans. As air transportation expanded, so did opportunities for hijacking.

Although the war ended in 1945, and U.S. and west European countries had free democratic governments, territory in east Europe was seized by the Soviet Union and turned into non-democratic communist states. The communist government in Moscow controlled the appointment of politicians in these east European countries liberated from Nazi rule but now under the yoke of communism. Many people in these countries wanted to escape **oppression** and **dictatorship**, and the first hijackings after World War II were carried out by people who were mostly seeking a means of escape.

The first of such acts was carried out in July 1947 when three Romanians killed an air crew member in an unsuccessful bid for

After World War II, military planes, like this Douglas Dakota, were used to carry passengers, ushering in the era of mass air transportation.

American hijacker Jack Graham (left) listens to testimony while on trial for the murder of his mother and 44 other people on a passenger plane in November 1955.

freedom. The Soviet secret police, the KGB, then put armed guards on flights flying close to the border with western Europe.

This did little to stop attempts at escape, and most of the 23 hijackings reported between 1947 and 1958 were due to escape attempts. There were many more that failed to get reported, and several Soviet aircraft were brought down by desperate people after gunfights in mid-air.

President and Mrs. Reagan greet former hostages of TWA flight 847 as they deplane at Andrews Air Force Base, in California, 1985.

Front of poster

A Defense Department release offers a reward of up to $25,000,000 for information leading to the arrest of Osama (or Usama) bin Laden (right) and Ayman (or Aiman) al-Zawahiri.

Back of of poster

PUSHTO

UP TO A $25,000,000 REWARD FOR INFORMATION LEADING TO THE WHEREABOUTS OR CAPTURE OF THESE TWO MEN.

DARI

UP TO A $25,000,000 REWARD FOR INFORMATION LEADING TO THE WHEREABOUTS OR CAPTURE OF THESE TWO MEN.

and to spread around the world. It purported to use the religion of Islam to justify violent acts of aggression, assassination, and mass murder. It would only be a matter of time before fanatics used airplanes as guided missiles to kill hundreds and thousands at a stroke.

During the 1990s a new group emerged and gathered strength among those willing to carry out mass murder. It was led by the Saudi Arabian Osama bin Laden, who was rejected by all Islamic countries including his own. The group known as Al Qaeda reached new levels of inhumanity and murder. From hideouts and training camps in Afghanistan, the organization planned mass murder on a scale never seen before.

From secret hideouts in Afghanistan Al Qaeda terrorists were trained for acts of violence around the world.

Chapter Five

The Events of September 11, 2001

The morning of September 11, 2001, was mild and cloudless with good weather predicted for all those flying out of U.S. east coast airports. On any given morning there are several hundred scheduled flights carrying commuters, businesspeople, civil servants, and general travelers. On this day four airliners would be hijacked, just as four had earlier been hijacked on one day in September of 1970. This time, the outcome would be very different, and it would change the world forever.

Of all the passengers on those flights, 19 men carried knowledge that if their plans worked as expected they would never see another sunset. About 7:00 a.m. five men with a special mission checked in at Boston's Logan airport for American Airlines flight 11 bound for Los Angeles. At another terminal another five men checked in for United Airlines flight 175 among other passengers also scheduled for Los Angeles.

At Washington-Dulles airport, at approximately the same time, five more men were among the passengers checking in for American Airlines flight 77 headed for Los Angeles. At Newark, New Jersey, four men joined fellow passengers aboard United Airlines flight 93 scheduled for San Francisco.

First to take off, at 7:59 a.m. from Boston-Logan, American Airlines flight 11 headed out for a non-stop flight across the country. The Boeing 767 carried 2 pilots, 9 flight attendants, and 81 passengers, including the 5 terrorists. About 15 minutes after takeoff the airliner had reached a height of 26,000 feet (7,925 m)

The remains of United Airlines Flight 175 at the site of the World Trade Center bombing, October 2001.

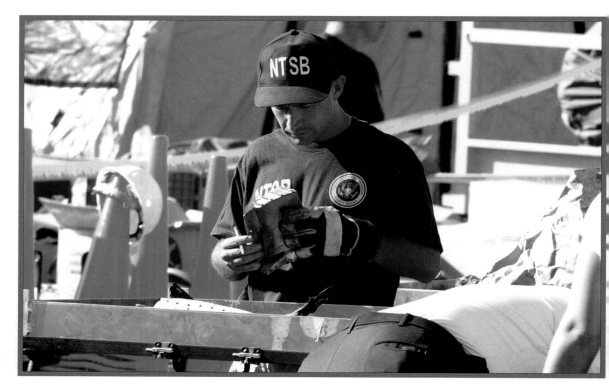

A National Transportation and Safety Board agent inspects and catalogs aircraft parts following the September 11, 2001 attacks on the Pentagon.

on its way to a cruising altitude of 35,000 feet (10,669 m). The "Fasten Seat Belt" sign was switched off, and the hijacking began.

Two men seated in first class stabbed two flight attendants, and access was gained to the flight deck where the two pilots were flying the airliner. Seconds later a third terrorist who had learned to fly the Boeing 767 entered the cockpit.

From the rear of the plane, flight attendant Madeline Sweeney calmly made a call to the ground and kept up a running commentary relaying what she could see as events unfolded. Betty Ong also used an air phone to contact the ground. Several passengers were stabbed as they tried to overwhelm the hijackers.

At 8:27 a.m., after a brief period of erratic flying, American 11 turned south and headed for New York City. Just before 8:47 a.m., the Boeing 767 carrying a total of 92 people was flown directly into the north tower of the World Trade Center,

President George W. Bush is told about the September 11 bombings while visiting a school in Sarasota, Florida.

immediately killing an unknown number in the building and starting catastrophic fires.

At about the time American 11 was being hijacked, United 175 with 2 pilots, 7 flight attendants, and 56 passengers aboard, took off from Boston-Logan and climbed to its assigned cruising altitude of 31,000 feet (9,449 m). At 8:42 a.m., the pilots monitored communication over the air waves about the hijacking of American 11 and then it was their turn. With 65 people on board, United 175 hit the south tower of the World Trade Center at 9:03 a.m.

Next off at 8:20 a.m. had been American 77, a Boeing 757 carrying 2 pilots, 4 flight attendants, and 58 passengers out of Washington-Dulles. Just over 30 minutes later, about 5 minutes after the first airliner crashed into the World Trade Center, American 77 too was taken over by the five suicide killers on board. It turned around and headed back toward Washington, crashing into the Pentagon seconds before 9:38 a.m.

Finally, at 8:42 a.m., United 93 took off from Newark-Liberty heading for San Francisco. The Boeing 757 was carrying 2 pilots, 5 flight attendants, and 37 passengers. This too was hijacked at around 9:28 a.m., about 10 minutes before American 77 hit the Pentagon.

What occurred on board United 93 will never be fully known. All that is certain is that an extraordinary effort was made by the passengers to retake control of the aircraft and prevent it hitting its intended target, now believed to have been the White House or the Capitol.

At 9:57 a.m. the passenger revolt began and was sustained for the remaining six minutes of flight. As the hijackers wrestled to keep control of the aircraft, the passengers began to overwhelm the four terrorists.

Several cell phone calls from United 93 relayed the sounds of frantic commotion, shouts, scuffles, and panic in the voices of the hijackers. With just 20 minutes flying time to the White House, the terrorists were only seconds from being overpowered. They screamed prayers to Allah (the Islamic name

The United States government responded quickly to the September 11 attacks by pounding Al Qaeda training camps in Afghanistan.

People from all over the world came to New York City for an observance ceremony one year after the September 11 bombings.

for God), rolled the aircraft on to its back, and plunged it into an empty field in Shanksville, Pennsylvania.

In all, 265 people aboard 4 airliners had taken off in a period of 43 minutes on a bright and sunny autumn morning. A little more than two hours later all four had crashed with total loss of life. Over the next few hours almost 3,000 more people died as a result of this single attack. They died at the Pentagon, and they died when the north and south towers of the World Trade Center collapsed. The world changed that day, and the world will never be the same again.

As a response to the threat from Al Qaeda and the terrible events of 9/11, the United States led a coalition to destroy the terrorist training camps and hideouts in Afghanistan. The United States established a new set of security standards and set up the Department of Homeland Security to coordinate the efforts of several separate U.S. departments and agencies. The U.S. government is working with allied governments around the world, but only time will tell if the efforts are enough to protect us from the scourge of terrorism.

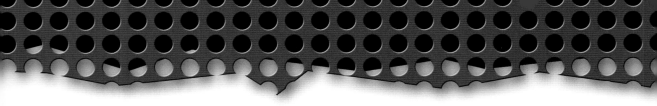

Glossary

catastrophic: describes a disastrous event

coerce: to persuade an unwilling person by using force or threats

dictatorship: a government run entirely by one person

escalating: increasing

freedom fighter: a person who takes part in violent action to overthrow an oppressive government

genocide: the killing of a large group of people, often of a particular race or nation

global: worldwide

guerrilla: a member of a small military group that carries out irregular fighting, often against larger forces

legitimate: something that is lawful or acceptable

oppression: the use of power in a cruel way

perpetrator: the person who is responsible for carrying out an action

principle: a basic rule that governs a person's behavior

refuge: a place of safety or shelter

sky marshal: an armed officer who travels on a plane disguised as an ordinary passenger

subservience: obeying orders without asking any questions

suppress: to put something down by force

surveillance: the close observation of something

uncompromising: describes someone who refuses to give in or change his or her mind

Further Reading

Binns, Tristan. *The CIA (Government Agencies)*. Sagebrush, 2002

Binns, Tristan. *The FBI (Government Agencies)*. Sagebrush, 2002

Brennan, Kristine. *The Chernobyl Nuclear Disaster (Great Disasters)*. Chelsea House, 2002

Campbell, Geoffrey A. *A Vulnerable America (Lucent Library of Homeland Security)*. Lucent, 2003

Donovan, Sandra. *How Government Works: Protecting America*. Lerner Publishing Group, 2004

Gow, Mary. *Attack on America: The Day the Twin Towers Collapsed (American Disasters)*. Enslow Publishers, 2002

Hasan, Tahara. *Anthrax Attacks Around the World (Terrorist Attacks)*. Rosen Publishing Group, 2003

Katz, Samuel M. *Global Counterstrike: International Counterterrorism (Terrorist Dossiers)*. Lerner Publishing Group, 2004

Katz, Samuel M. *Targeting Terror: Counterterrorist Raids (Terrorist Dossiers)*. Lerner Publishing Group, 2004

Katz, Samuel M. *U.S. Counterstrike: American Counterterrorism (Terrorist Dossiers)*. Lerner Publishing Group, 2004

Margulies, Phillip. *Al-Qaeda: Osama Bin Laden's Army of Terrorists (Inside the World's Most Infamous Terrorist Organizations)*. Rosen Publishing Group, 2003

Marquette, Scott. *America Under Attack (America at War)*. Rourke Publishing LLC, 2003

Morris, Neil. *The Atlas of Islam*. Barron's, 2003

Owen, David. *Hidden Secrets: A Complete History of Espionage and the Technology Used to Support It*. Firefly Books Ltd, 2002

Ritchie, Jason. *Iraq and the Fall of Saddam Hussein*. Oliver Press, 2003

Websites to visit

The Central Intelligence Agency:
www.cia.gov

The Department of Defense:
www.defenselink.mil

The Department of Homeland Security:
www.dhs.gov

The Federal Bureau of Investigation:
www.fbi.gov

The U.S. Air Force:
www.af.mil

The U.S. Army
www.army.mil

The U.S. Coast Guard:
www.uscg.mil

The U.S. Government Official Website:
www.firstgov.gov

The U.S. Marine Corps:
www.usmc.mil

The U.S. Navy:
www.navy.mil

The U.S. Secret Service:
www.secretservice.gov

The White House:
www.whitehouse.gov

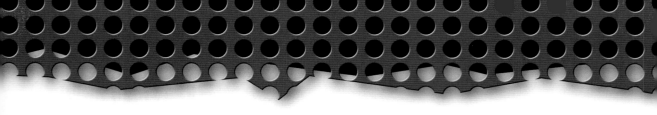

Index